ali's world

ali's world

BADAL & SWAPNA MUKHOPADHYAY

Foreword by
AAMIR KHAN

Lustre Press
Roli Books

Cover
Collage, 1997
Poster colour on canvas
921 x 1220

Cover (inside)
Untitled, December, 1998
Ink on paper

Facing page
The Boy, 1988
Poster colour on paper
210 x 290

Contents

Foreword	7
Where Do I Start?	8
Acknowledgements	87
List of Plates	92

Plate 01
Untitled
(Red Balls and Blue)

Foreword

The loss of a near and dear one is heartbreaking, and I do not want to pretend to be able to fully appreciate the pain, as only those who go through it face it, and somehow find the strength to live with it.

My heart goes out to Badal and Swapna, and as a parent I can only try and hold their hand and pass on whatever warmth that I can. The fact that my film touched a chord with Badal and Swapna is something I feel blessed about. And from whatever I can gather you both have done a wonderful job of giving him a happy life.

In many ways the story of Ali is close to each of ours, and in many ways it is unique.

When I see Ali's work I am mesmerized. I feel moved by what I see. His paintings engage and enrich me. My reaction to his work is not a result of any sympathy, as when I first saw the book I had no idea of his background, or his tragic and untimely end. It was only when I went through the book for the second time, read the text and the accompanying letter that I felt a sense of loss. I am not an expert on art but I just loved his work. It gets you in the gut and speaks to you, moves you.

I think Ali has managed to communicate in his short life more than most of us do in three times the life span. Certainly by the time I was 20 I had not even begun to express myself. His work, and I hesitate to call it that as it comes across more as play to me, seems to celebrate every aspect of his life. My congratulations to Ali, and thank you, Badal and Swapna, for giving us a peek into his world.

Aamir Khan

When this book was nearly ready, we happened to watch Aamir Khan's hugely acclaimed movie, *Taare Zameen Par.* The film tells the story of a dyslexic child who is encouraged by his teacher to follow his dream of becoming an artist. We were mesmerised. It resonated with our memories of raising Ali. On an impulse, we sent Mr. Khan a pre-publication copy of the book. He responded by writing this Foreword. How do we thank him? We have no clue.

— Badal and Swapna Mukhopadhyay

Where Do I Start?

I do not know where to start.

The shining stars in the university gardens, blinking at me, winking at me. Which one of these are you, baby? Which one? Walk, walk, walk, walk. Are you okay, baby? Must be! Or else why would you shine so bright? Why would you smile so bright? Some day, some time, I will catch up with you. Until then, just walk, walk, walk, walk … until you are exhausted.

If only I knew which one of those you are! The brightest one, no? The best boy in the whole big world?

That day they brought over a bundle to me. I was exhausted. Could barely breathe. They brought over the bundle to show me. I can remember the eyes – the bright blue eyes. Sky-blue eyes. Lack of oxygen, they told me. How did he survive? Later, I saw him again, when I could stand and walk. I walked to the intensive care unit and saw him again. A tiny little thing – red and wrinkled. Like a cut up chicken. He could not breathe properly. Could not suck. He had to be kept there, they said. You go back home, they said. Is he going to survive? Yes, he will, they said. I will call him Arpan, I thought. I will give him over to You. You saved him. He is Yours. Look after him. Please …

So He did. He took him away. I cannot complain. How can I complain?

Where do I start?

—Ma

Plate 02
Untitled, 1998
Ink on paper
1157 x 1153

ALI was born eight weeks premature. I recall waiting on the staircase in the old St. Stephen's Hospital ward, counting seconds. In those days there was nowhere to sit. Swapna was inside.

What was happening?

Plate 03
Man and Machine, 1994
Mixed media on paper
28 x 49

Since the morning, Swapna had felt reduced foetal movement, so she went to see her obstetrician, Dr Kavan, at St. Stephen's Hospital. The doctor detected foetal distress. Throughout Ali's life, Swapna's intuition about him proved right. Dr Kavan performed immediate surgery under local anaesthesia because Swapna was just coming out of an asthma attack, which ruled out general anaesthesia. It was horrendously painful because standard painkillers could not be administered. But in the end, both mother and child were safe.

After what seemed to be a very long time, a visiting German nurse came out with a bundle in her arms. 'Did it cry?' I asked excitedly. She began unravelling the bundle, saying, 'It's a boy!' Then I heard a strange sound and I nearly screamed when comprehension dawned and she said, 'Yes, yes, he's crying!' I was looking at a tiny creature, with a big head and large bluish eyes. We later learnt that the blue of the eyes indicated a lack of adequate oxygen.

A few years later, Dr Kavan died of cancer. The children's wing of St. Stephens' Hospital has since been renamed the 'S. Kavan' wing.

We left Ali at the hospital's intensive care unit and came home. Two days later, my cousin, a doctor, walked in holding a favourite fish preparation for Swapna, expecting her to be seven months pregnant at that time. He nearly collapsed when he heard the news !

Plate 04
***Untitled*, 1994**
Mixed media on paper
37 x 55

It became a routine for us to go to the hospital everyday and peer through the intensive care unit's glass window at this unbelievably small creature, who blinked in the light, protesting at being disturbed. But we could not hear any sound.

Three weeks later, when Swapna returned to the hospital to learn how to handle a premature baby, we learnt to identify his cry. It was shriller and yet less audible than the chirping of a newly hatched chick. His huge head, with its two large blue eyes, had a mouth so small that we had to use a dropper to feed him. His resistance levels were so low, we were told, that at home we would have to quarantine him. Whoever handled him could touch nothing else.

Fortunately, we had one bedroom with an attached bath and a small six-by-four foot alcove. We found a frail old Nepalese woman to help Swapna to tend the baby and sleep on a cot in the quarantined room. After six weeks she was a wreck because she had to wake up at all hours.

But contrary to our fears, our baby lived. His mother named him 'Arpan', an offering to God. I forecast that he would be big, strong and generous, like the only person I hero-worshipped while at graduate school in the United States. I called him Ali.

RPAN

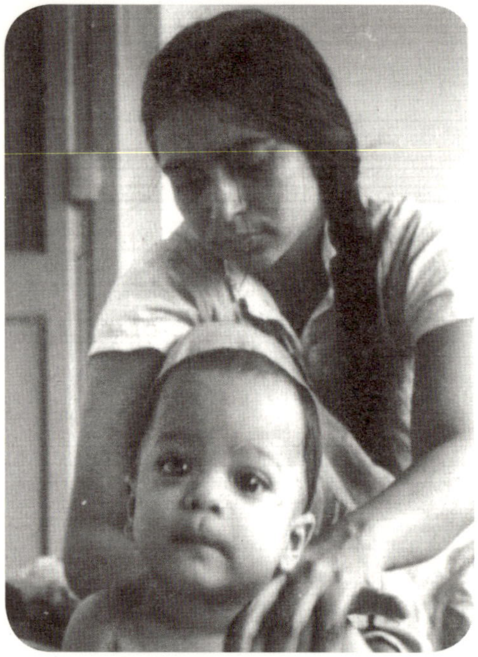

In the meanwhile, our older son, Anirban (we called him Buju at home), four years old at the time, diligently scribbled, 'It my baby brother is small. Do not enter' on all the outer walls of Ali's room.

The baby brother grew, although he started to talk, and walk, late. But by the time he was about two years old, his body was still tiny, his head large and, we realized, his legs strong. He wanted to run before he could even walk. It was a peculiar run, wobbly and unbalanced. It seemed as if he would fall any moment, but he did not. He moved a bit like Charlie Chaplin – bending left, bending right, stumbling on one foot, then on the other, disappearing from sight round the corner, and reappearing in a flash.

Once, when the grand patriarch of Indian economics, Professor V.K.R.V. Rao, came to dinner, Ali took an instant fancy to him. He decided to entertain our visitor. He ran into the living room, clambered on top of a low wooden table in front of Professor Rao, jumped twice, climbed down, ran out at great speed, ran back in two minutes, and then repeated the whole performance all over again. Professor Rao could not stop laughing.

When a visitor came for a chat and he took out a fresh pack of cigarettes from his pocket, Ali pleaded for the cellophane wrap, which he got immediately. He sat on the next sofa and went on to tear off little pieces, crumpling them up into little balls and kept on giving them to our guest, claiming them to be what he had just discovered the beauty of – homoeopathic pills. What the unsuspecting man did not see was that in order to hold the balls in place, Ali was spitting on them to prevent them from opening up.

One trait of Ali's surfaced pretty early. On the lawns of the staff quarters of the Institute of Economic Growth (IEG), where Swapna was working at the time, he would chase a ball thrown for our dog Buchi, like a maniac. Of course Buchi would reach it first, but would bring it back and drop it at his feet. At times she would

Plate 05
Tree and the Sun, 1994
Watercolour on paper

simply stand by the ball, dripping saliva on it, waiting for Ali to come and pick it up. This great Labrador would tolerate everything from Ali. On the same lawns too we found out that he was making friends with all the other kids, some much older than himself, with great alacrity.

So, barring the worries of our paediatrician friend, Dr Sarla Khanvilkar, who would measure the circumference of his head with a tape on every visit, Ali grew well. His oddities were yet to be revealed.

Growing Up

At about this time, we faced another anxiety on a different front. Once Ali started to run before he walked, he seemed to develop a keen attraction for our old music system: a Garrard turntable, a Sony 7-½" spool player, a Sherwood amplifier, and so on. For a while, we parked it in a corner room, which was locked whenever we were away. But this proved rather inconvenient. So, we got hold of a competent carpenter who made us a single cabinet with compartments for the turntable, the spool player, the amplifier, etc. with interconnections through apertures to the rear. Each cabinet was secured with a Godrej lock. Ali did not like this one bit. A week later, we returned home to discover that while our cook was making *chapati*s, Ali kept running in, begging for dough to make his own *chapati*s. In good faith, and to buy peace, the cook had obliged. Little did he realize that each lump of dough was being stuck into a keyhole of the cabinet. Ali ruined all the keyholes!

'As kids, whenever our parents would go abroad, they'd bring back chocolates, which would be put into the fridge. I was always of the opinion that if we ate them slooooowly, we'd have them for longer. He was always of the opinion that a chocolate not eaten is not a chocolate. Hence within a couple of days, he'd have finished off all of them, and I would barely have tasted a few.'

—*Anirban (Buju)*

The Two Brothers in Bangkok

In 1980, we went to Bangkok for a few months and discovered that even though our kids were six plus and two plus, there were things about them that we knew nothing of. Perhaps they did not either.

First, food. How much those two, of which one was a mere toddler, could eat was mind-boggling! By the time I reached office, they would have eaten a hefty breakfast and were getting ready to go swimming in the pool of the apartment complex. By this time, Swapna would have shoved in a cake to bake in the oven. By 11.00 a.m. there would be no cake left! Not even a crumb. By midday, the two boys were inside the bath-tub, Ali with his rubber duckies. By 1.00 p.m., out of the bath, they would settle down to a hearty lunch. By 3.30 p.m. or so I would return home and they would be waiting to have snacks with me! By 4.30 p.m. we were all out of the house, walking and eating.

Our elder son began to resemble a fat puppy in no time, but not Ali. Even in the small round pool in the apartment complex, he used to squirm about like a fish, burning energy. He just moved and moved and moved!

The second thing we discovered was a maniacal fascination for clothes. In those days, Bangkok had wonderful street markets for clothes and we bought heaps of those for the two kids. Buju would sombrely walk up to his drawer, carefully choose one and go away to wear it. Not Ali. Whichever one we picked for him was the wrong one and he would howl away in misery, tears streaming down his cheeks, 'No, no, this is not my nice shirt!' It would take us an hour to get out of the house, even to visit friends next door, because Ali needed time to dress up.

Shiv Niketan

Back in Delhi, we decided that Ali was old enough (and trouble enough at home) – it was time for him to go to a nursery school. The day he turned three years old, we took him to Shiv Niketan on Hailey Road. Buju was already a student there and so were the children of many of our friends. This was a school unlike any other we knew: no pressure, no exams, no grades.

But the beginning was difficult. About a dozen or more kids would be crammed into a taxi from our neighbourhood taxi service. The taxi was driven in turns by two very gentle and caring Sikh drivers, Gurnam Singh and Talwar Singh. But, in summer and in the monsoons, it was very uncomfortable inside the taxi, and Ali hated it. Every day, when the taxi returned and the door opened, we found him sitting on the edge of the back seat with his head lodged on the back of the driver's seat, sleeping. I would shudder at the thought of him hurting his neck, little realizing how strong the kid was growing to be.

Ali would bring home report cards that read: 'He likes to doodle on the floor with chalk. He likes to smell orange-scented erasers.' One wondered how the teachers ever found out. Through the years, the school principal, who was universally referred to as Aunty Gauba, and her fantastic team of teachers, would urge the children to work on original plays that they would themselves script, provide background music to and, eventually, stage. This, as we realized later, was an environment wonderful for all kinds of kids, but vital for Ali.

He was about three years old and showing every sign of his sweet tooth. No chocolate, *rasgoola* or *laddoo* would remain for a day in the fridge – Ali ate them all. So, my father tried to teach him to do penance; he would have to say a prayer before he would get a sweet.

'He likes to doodle on the floor with chalk and smell orange-scented erasers.'

—Teacher at Shiv Niketan

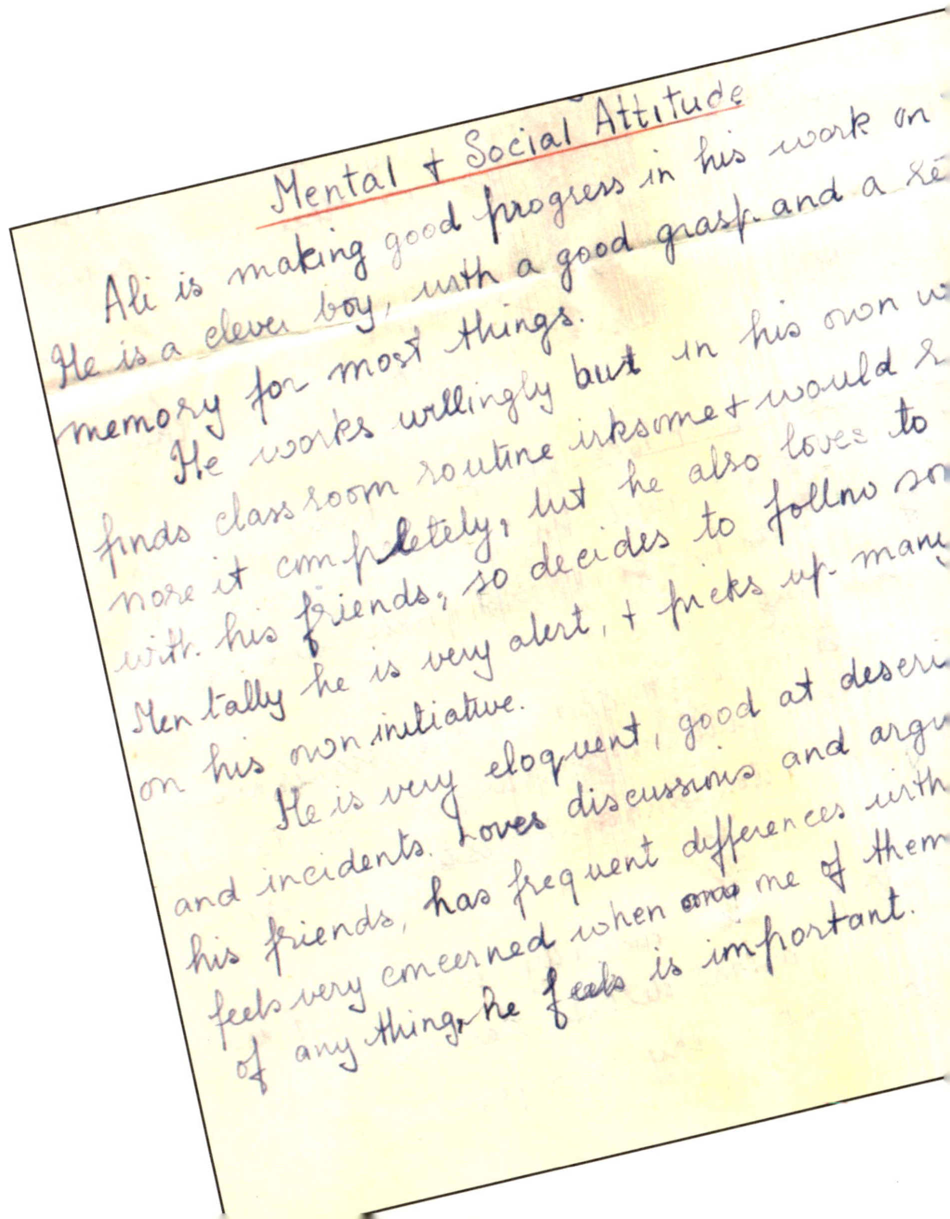
Mental + Social Attitude
Ali is making good progress in his work on
He is a clever boy, with a good grasp. and a re
memory for most things.
He works willingly but in his own w
finds class room routine irksome + would
more it completely, but he also loves to
with his friends, so decides to follow so
Mentally he is very alert, + picks up many
on his own initiative.
He is very eloquent, good at descri
and incidents. Loves discussions and argu
his friends, has frequent differences with
feels very concerned when one of them
of anything he feels is important.

Disaster followed. We were visiting a friend who, after a while, fetched a bowl of *rasgoola*s from her kitchen. As she walked towards the table Ali's head was turning with a fixed stare at it, and he was shouting, 'I am a sinner, I am a sufferer, Oh Thou Supreme Lord, please forgive me.' (In Bengali '*Ami Papi, Ami Tapi. Oh Parampita Parameshwar, Amaake tumi Kshama Karo*'). Our friend almost dropped the bowl in surprise.

Meanwhile, Ali was getting to be naughtier by the day. He seemed to know that he could get away with murder, thanks to his cherubic face and innocent smile. His pranks multiplied, keeping our household permanently on tenterhooks. There were far too many to recall all of them, but here is an example.

This episode is told with hindsight. There was a much bigger, older Sikh girl in Shiv Niketan who complained every day at home about this naughty youngster, Ali, who troubled her in school so much that she did not want to go to school. Her father decided to tell the teachers nothing but to find out what was happening for himself. So he arrived at the school one morning and asked one of the teachers who Ali was and whether he could meet the blighter. Out walked this youngster, still small for his years, and knowing fully well what might be in store, bestowing his sweetest innocent look on the gentleman. The Sardarji stared, gulped, gave him as wide a return smile as he could muster, wheeled around and gave his daughter a resounding slap! The girl burst into tears.

When we heard of this episode, I remember looking for the nearest curtain to hide behind.

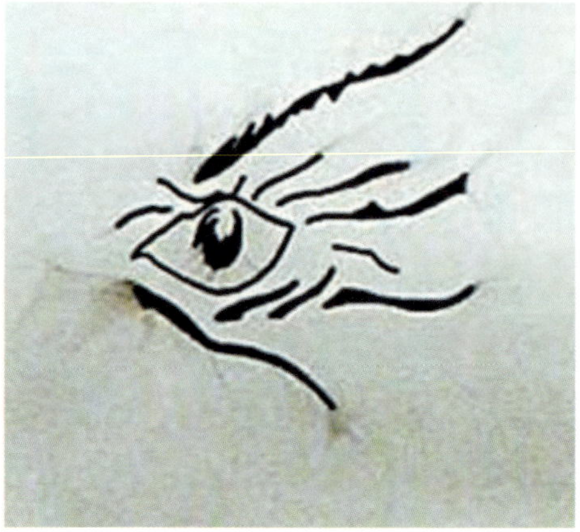

Sketch
Eye

Ali was nearly four when we went to celebrate the annual day of the Presidency College alumni in Delhi. This was very much the affair of our civil servant (Indian Administrative Service) friends. Packed into two buses, we descended on a beautiful resort in Haryana.

There were some events organized for the kids, including an egg-in-the-spoon race. The kids had to run fifty metres holding a spoon in their teeth and the egg was on the spoon. The idea was not to spill it.

I recall trying to prevent Ali from participating for somehow I was sure that he would cheat, but my IAS friends who catch cheats in the whole country, laughed and got him to join. Ali sprinted away and won the race with the second kid nearly twenty metres behind. Here is the next conversation.

'Ali, what did you do?'
'Nothing, absolutely.'
'Stop lying. You cheated, and now you are lying too.'
Silence.
'WHAT DID YOU DO?'
'I smiled.'
'What?'
'See, when you smile you pucker your cheeks and so, I could hold the egg between the spoon and my left cheek.'

'As an eight-year-old, he broke into the luggage of our visitors from abroad and took out a whole carton of (I think) Marlboros. That's not the point – the point is that he shared them out with all the other eight-year-olds on campus.

—*Anirban (Buju)*

Plant
Watercolour

Kuala Lumpur

Early in 1983, Swapna and I took the kids for another stay abroad – this time in Kuala Lumpur. The kids settled down to their routine at a new school, and spent the rest of their time with toys and games, making endless visits to shopping malls and eating places. Around this time, it became clear that although Ali was not keen on books, he was extremely good with his hands, be it the computer games which the two boys would play endlessly, or other toys that needed dexterity. Ali could handle them all with great speed.

There was one toy in which a large plastic cube had different shapes of apertures cut on all sides and the task was to recognize which object would go through which slot. This Ali would do with great speed. Swapna was still worried about any brain damage due to premature birth and so we went to see a renowned child specialist. She confronted Ali with that toy and in two minutes pronounced him to be perfectly okay. She was wrong.

Those days, computer games were not yet universal. South-east Asia was the market for the Nintendo brands; our kids had two. One was hand-held and by using only the two thumbs you had to help two monkeys load cartons on to a delivery truck. Each successful loading would be accompanied by a short shrill 'bleep'. The other was a bigger game to be played with joysticks.

Almost every morning when I woke up, I heard a continuous 'bleep, bleep, bleep' coming from the living room. There, lying on his tummy on the carpet was Ali loading those cartons with both hands with incredible speed.

But the bigger game took longer and usually involved other kids. Once my cousin, Rina, visited us from the UK with her husband and daughter, who was about the age of our older son, about ten years old. Come evening and they were all on the carpet in the living room shooting down those UFOs. It was a warm summer evening and the kids were consuming coke by the gallons. Eventually we had to stop them for dinner. At the table, we started sensing a funny smell somewhere. In his anxiety not to miss the game, but also eager for the coke, Ali had been running out to piddle in the balcony adjoining the living room – all evening!

Sydney

In late 1984, Swapna gave up her United Nations job at Kuala Lumpur. We moved to Sydney, where she and I had invitations to teach at the university. The kids were admitted to the Forest Lodge School in Glebe. In the kindergarten, the teachers caried out the practice of putting a rubber stamp with 'Best Student Today' on the reverse of the left palm of one student every day. We still do not know what Ali did to charm his teacher, but every other day he would come home with that stamp all over him – hands, legs, back, tummy, bottom, everywhere!

One of our colleagues, Louis Haddad and his wife Salem had four kids, the youngest a little younger than Ali. Every other weekend, all of us drove into the countryside for a bush walk. The six kids were sent out to gather sticks and branches for the barbeque, at which Louis was an expert. Back in Sydney, with Louis' help, I had to set up a makeshift barbeque unit in our small backyard to meet the children's demands. Impelled by the smoky wood smell and fantastic Australian meat, the barbeque never failed. The kids would eat kilos at each sitting.

The Los Angeles Olympics took place in 1984. Television channels were relaying sports events round the clock. When Ali saw a kid doing a sidewise cartwheel on one show, he went berserk. Fortunately, our living room floor had a heavy rug, so he did not break any bones. He would do a sidewise cartwheel by himself for hours on end and in no time at all, had mastered it perfectly.

Ali in the News!

Returning from the university one afternoon around Christmas time, Swapna and I were surprised to find Ali's photograph prominently displayed in the local daily called *Glebe Times* under a banner headline:

ARPAN SAYS, 'JESUS WAS A KING BABY.' …

It appeared that a reporter had visited our children's school to ask the kids what they thought Christmas was all about. As usual, Ali took the lead in responding. His conversation with the reporter went thus:

Sketch
Mother Teresa
Ink on paper

'…We tried out so many things together …. We were nine when we first hitched a ride together, despite dire warnings from a third, more law-abiding friend; we were thirteen when we first went to a restaurant alone; fifteen when we drank together, and so on across many years. In most contexts, rebellion or at least the frisson or feeling of it, or the desire of it, was the highest principle for Ali.'

—Bhrigu

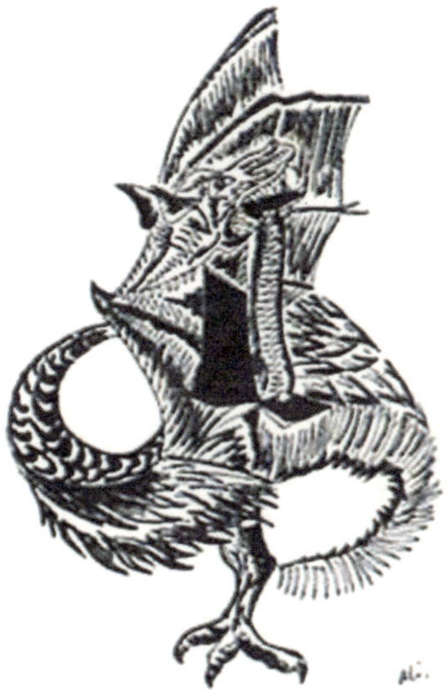

Sketch : ***Dragon***

Reporter : 'Why is Christmas so important?'
Ali : 'Because it is the birthday of Jesus.'
Reporter : 'Who was Jesus?'
Ali : 'Jesus was a baby.'
Reporter : 'But why was he so great?'
Ali : 'Because he was a King Baby.'

A fanciful description of how good a kid he was at home followed. As parents, we knew better!

We often had to feed large contingents of neighbourhood kids invited by Ali to share our meals, while we had no clue about how many of them were likely to arrive or when. We simply had to get used to this pattern of having a large number of unexpected guests! Until the end, we never knew how many of Ali's friends were invited for a meal on any particular day.

Plate 06
Detail from 'The Puppies'
November, 1998
Acrylic on canvas and serigraphy
900 x 590

Sketch
***A Woman*, 1994**
Ink on paper

Were we Wrong?

We returned to Delhi in early 1985. Ali was six-plus, and still had to wait a while before middle school. So, we went back to Shiv Niketan and Aunty Gauba.

I do not know when we began to make mistakes with Ali, but it might have been from this time. Aunty Gauba asked him to write a page of anything he wanted to. He promptly produced a page of gibberish, which would have earned him congratulatory rubber stamps at Forest Lodge. Aunty Gauba reacted with anger. She insisted there had to be a minimum of discipline in any individual and we could see her point.

But Ali was not like most other kids. In fact, as it turned out, he was very different. How do parents and teachers recognize this when the kid is only six years old? Were the teachers in Australia, who gave Ali an absolutely free run, better at their job? Should we have let him be a free spirit, running the risk of getting nowhere? We will never know.

Ali spent one more year at Shiv Niketan, but he was much bigger, stronger and naughtier than he was at three, when he had started going to the school. He would regularly eat up other kids' lunches at school, while his own remained untouched. At home, we had permanent trouble with maids and helping hands.

Ali, a Handful!

He would return home by about 2.30 p.m., while Buju was still at school. Swapna would be at her office at the IEG campus, while I was at the Delhi School of Economics. So, an adult was needed at home to keep Ali out of trouble. We hired a big, strong young cook from Bihar.

Once, in the height of summer, Ali stayed back from school, pleading a stomach ache. At around 11 a.m., he turned up at Swapna's office at the IEG. Her colleagues pampered him and let him stay on. Back home for lunch, Swapna found Ali had locked up the poor Bihari chap inside the bathroom, bolting its door. Climbing onto a chair, he had unlocked the front door and set out to visit his mother. The cook stewed inside for two hours, cried buckets, and promptly left for his village once he was rescued.

On another occasion, Ali came home with a friend, had lunch, and told the maid they would play in the bedroom. When she left, the two proceeded to set newspapers on fire. When the flames rose too high for comfort, they shoved the whole mess under a box bed. By the time we returned, the room was a pool of water!

Mrs Desai, our neighbour downstairs, was the kindest of souls. One evening, while Swapna and she were having tea on her lawn, they saw the tiny figure of Ali shooting in and out of her house. Ali, who had no communication with Mrs Desai, had nevertheless no compunction about darting into her house, climbing onto her kitchen counters and reaching for the cookie jars. He knew they were filled with wonderful goodies from her daughter in faraway Kabul. He would grab as much as he could, then disappear in a flash. While Swapna was enormously embarrassed, Mrs Desai finally understood why her stock of sweets was dwindling at such an inexplicably high rate. So were the tomatoes from her garden, which served Ali as balls to play with.

Ali was constantly in trouble. The first time he broke an arm he was barely six years old. It was only a green-stick fracture, but it did need a plaster. Very soon the plaster was signed all over by friends. A couple of days later, the plaster became soggy. We discovered that Ali was using it on his 'enemies'. We rushed him back to the orthopaedist who was shocked at the damage and had to redo the plaster.

Once when Ali got a bad cut on his left knee, I had to drive him to my doctor cousin in Netaji Nagar every night for a change of dressing. The wound started to heal and he was told not to play until he was completely cured. Sure enough, he did not obey, and got hurt in the same place again. There was a risk of bone damage – and this time he had to pay attention – and was sidelined for a month.

'I have inherited a lifetime of memories from those nine months of companionship. The two of us were very different people, but for some reason, we got along like we had known each other from another lifetime. From the very beginning of our friendship, conversations were never important – we'd enjoy just being with each other. Yes, I can say maybe we were in love.'

—Surya

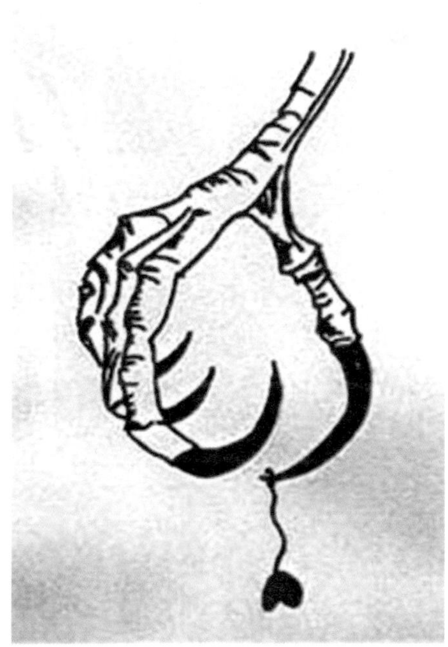

Sketch
Claw

A Congenitally Generous Child!

On the IEG campus, Ali was the darling of all the children around. Without batting an eyelid, he would take money from our wallets, lead the kids across a fairly dangerous road intersection near our home, and buy them chocolates. And, of course, with equal fluency, he would lie through his teeth. By now, it was becoming clear that his attention was not just chocolate-centric. He would give away almost anything that looked interesting – toys, torches, pens, shoe-horns, just about anything bright and shiny would disappear at great speed.

Our Thirty-one Points Child

In the summer of 1987, we went to Kolkata. In the previous winter, Ali had watched Buju, Swapna, my father and I play contract bridge and his eyes gleamed. So I taught him the basics: four suits, the cards, the point count and the simplest of bids. This time in Kolkata, my father would eagerly wait to sit with his two grandchildren and me and tolerate all possible blunders. But Ali had trouble counting points while holding the cards in his hand, so he turned his back to us, and spread the cards out to count. But when he turned back again, his guileless face revealed quite a bit about his hand, and I always scolded him. One particular day in one deal, when he turned back, he was beaming and this angered me. I shouted at him and threw my cards down. Tears started streaming down his face, he cried, 'But I had thirty-one points!'

Hundreds of times later when we played, I would silently pray 'get thirty-one points, get thirty-one points' – but he never did. Nor will he ever.

Sketch

For Vini Didi

Sketch
***Buchi*, 1997**
Serigraphy
255 x 197

Football

At Springdales School on Pusa Road, where Buju studied, Ali was a misfit. Unlike the others, Buju and his friends, he was not a 'good student'. Besides, he was very naughty. We began getting, and dreading, summons from his school. Ali's grade card was a saw-tooth. Every time Swapna worked with him, his grades went up, only to drop once again when he was on his own. But we found out two significant facts. Ali still liked to doodle, and he still chased a ball on the ground madly.

So, we paid attention to these side activities – making it possible for him to play football, and getting him to an art school somewhere. Ali's dexterity with the football had surfaced pretty early.

Springdales had an inter-class football tournament. Anyone who played for his class team, could compete in the tournament. I routinely drove Ali to the school field before class hours when matches were played. With no Buchi around, he was clearly one of the quickest with the ball on the field.

Under the Springdales sports teacher and football coach, Mr Kapoor, Ali was growing to be a good sportsman, a fine striker in football. I remember the time when Ali was playing for Springdales in an inter-school competition. Swapna and I had promised to come and watch him play. But we were late and arrived only at half-time. The match was at nil-nil. Mr Kapoor was livid when we came to the field, but Ali saw us and broke into his cherubic smile.

Over the next fifteen minutes, he scored three goals, the last with two defenders from the other side and their goalkeeper hanging on to him. Ali walked with the whole team into the net in triumph. He was in Class XI then and very strong.

'I recollect memories of laughter, tantrums, tears, happiness, from childhood and adolescence ... the muscular artist is pretty much the same as the sweet kid of a decade back, and I know that my memories of Ali ... will live on, as real as the paintings he has left behind.'

—Advaith

Painting: The Beginnings

For painting, we first sent Ali to the Delhi University Women's Association, near our home. Then, there were art classes at his school.

It dawned on us that he was pretty skilled with his doodles when he was about ten years old. Springdales School had just appointed a young artist named Kadambari as an assistant librarian. She was very good with the children (they called her Cadbury) – and she took Ali under her wing.

One day, Swapna discovered a sketch of an African boy's face in his schoolbag. Could Kadambari have drawn it? 'Of course not,' said Ali indignantly, 'Kadambari would have done a much better sketch.' We thought it was wonderful. Swapna promptly got it framed and that face has adorned our sitting room ever since. We knew then that Ali would have to concentrate on art as a major subject.

Sketch
The Boy
Poster-colour

Lack of Adjustment at School

While his love for football and painting continued, Ali's inability to settle down at school was becoming increasingly pronounced. The dissonance with authority grew almost in proportion to his popularity among his friends. On his school-leaving day, his juniors voted him Mr Springdales, the most popular senior on campus. But he irritated an increasing number of his teachers. Some complained that they would turn around from the blackboard to find that Ali had sneaked out of the class through the back door. Others compared him with Buju, who was good in studies, despite our appeals to them to desist from comparing the two brothers. Complaints kept pouring in. We often had to do a difficult balancing act between answering his teachers and asking Ali to behave better. Only a few teachers loved the essential child in him – and that love was reciprocated many times over.

Thus emerged the adolescent who had stormy relations with just about everybody, great friendships alternating with angry exchanges. The only one spared was our splendid Labrador, Buchi. Their mutual love never failed. All through Ali's school years, Buchi would sit on the balcony ledge like a tiger every afternoon, waiting for the school bus to return. Then, as she

'When he had money, he spent it on friends, when he ran out, he borrowed. It was the same with everything he owned – music, clothes, books ... He didn't always know who had borrowed what from his room. I'm not sure it mattered. He just felt good sharing.'

— ***Advaith***

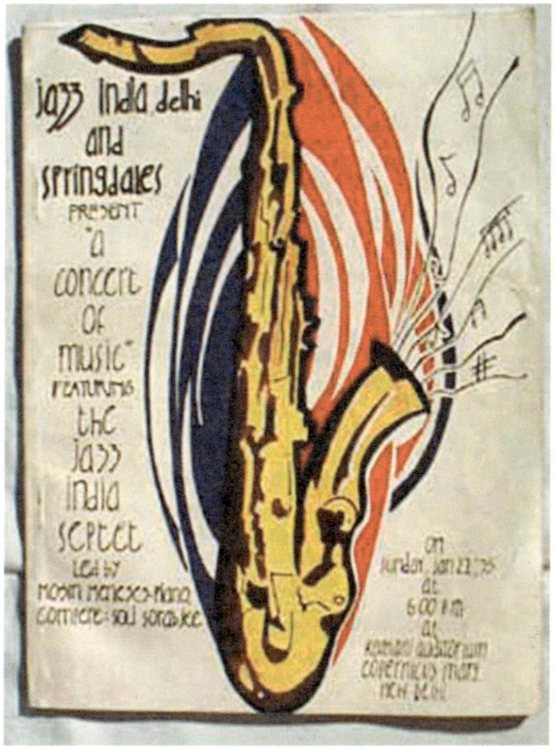

Poster
College Fest

watched him approach our house, she would roar. As soon as Ali walked in, she would jump on him. The two would roll about on the floor for a few minutes and then, they would get up and go their separate ways; at last, peace would descend. This scene was repeated every single school day.

There was another ritual enacted almost daily. It was simply impossible to wake Ali up in the mornings, until Buju worked out a solution. At the command of, 'Buchi, Ali up!' this great dog would jump onto his bed and start licking his nose. No matter how deeply you are asleep, you are unlikely to enjoy this for too long, with forty kilograms of weight over you. Screams and kicks would follow. Then, Buchi with a wagging tail, would demand her regulation reward of a biscuit.

Ali and his Friends

Ever since he was a child, Ali was committed to friends. He had no enemy. He was there for his friends under all conceivable circumstances, with no holds barred. He was virtually bed-ridden with broken bones when his friend Bhrigu's father was hospitalized, but he turned a deaf ear to all medical advice. We had to rush him to the hospital, so that he could be with his friend in his time of grief. Tara, another dear friend and senior in school, could freely call him at any hour, to fetch class notes from friends lodged at various hostels on the campus, before her final exams. Ali would happily mount his bike and shoot out into the night if she needed him.

'It was my eighteenth birthday party. Ali, who was usually the life and soul of get-togethers, just sat in my rocking chair for most of the time without saying a word, looking very morose, and then left. These are fairly unexciting things to recall about someone who was never boring, but I think they are as indicative as anything else of what he was like.'

—Tara

FRIDAY 15th JAN '99. 3:45.

Graffiti on Ali's
bedroom wall
Almost Famous
15 January, 1999

‘His paintings keep coming back to me, they just describe him so well, even as I struggle to find the right words. Free thinking, creative, genuine, reckless, gentle, in his art, his soccer, his life. ... His recklessness was often infuriating, but then recklessness just seems to go hand in hand with extreme creativity.’

Advaith

Plate 07
Heart of the Sun
April, 1998
Acrylic and ink on canvas
915 x 1220

'Ali had described this picture to his friends as the image of a woman who has just been hit by pot. She sees herself floating above and all of nature is below her. I loved it when he finished painting it and called it his 'Lucy in the Sky' picture. I forced Ali to gift it to me and had it hanging in my office.'

—***Swapna***

Plate 08
The Pot Plant
(Lucy in the Sky)
1998
355 x 520

Dyslexia

As a child grows up through middle school to high school, then college, and beyond, he or she spends less time at home every day, and more and more outside. The parents of all kids down the middle of the road accept this. But some parents must be prepared for the exception: not better, not worse, but simply different. It was in middle school at Springdales that problems due to Ali's premature birth eventually surfaced, first spotted by a sensitive teacher. In class, Ali would sit at the rear and never really pay attention. One day, this lady sent us a note, suggesting that we might want to get his hearing checked. We did, immediately. Ali was found to be at least thirty per cent deficient in the hearing frequencies which people normally speak in. We got him a hearing aid which, after some time, disappeared. He had given it away!

But the more serious problem was detected slightly later. Early one morning, Swapna woke me up, urging me to read an article on dyslexia in the morning paper. Unlike now, dyslexia was a disorder rarely heard about in those days. The doctor who had written it had listed its common symptoms. They were: confusion of 'b' and 'd', 'p' and 'q'; skipping words while reading; inability to perform simple arithmetical calculations and so on. Ali had almost all of them. Swapna's intuition proved right again.

We reached for the phone. My cousin, who was a medical doctor, advised us to immediately consult Dr Puri at the Rajkumari Amrit Kaur Centre. I recall that Dr Puri sat in a room with a large glass panel on one side, beyond which was another room full of children's toys and games. Ali had come with us straight from school in his uniform. He put his satchel down and was chatting and playing with some younger kids. We were made to fill up a detailed form that Dr Puri read. When she looked up, she began, 'Let's see, there may be a problem.' Then she saw Ali, and stopped.

'Is this the boy?'

'Yes.'

'Can't be!'

Plate 09
Untitled
610 x 455

She called him in, spoke to him for some time, and sent him for an IQ test. Ali got a pretty good score, but in a peculiar manner. There were large blocks that he did 100 per cent right, while others were all wrong. In the end, her prognosis was: nothing seems to be seriously wrong, but we had to be 'careful' with this kid. That was easier said than done. What exactly were we supposed to do, or not do?

We hunted up the author of the original article and took an appointment with her. In this lady's clinic, the condition of the other dyslexic kids scared us. Most were very quiet, withdrawn, staring blankly at nothing. It seemed unbelievable that Ali – bubbly, full of naughtiness, fun and life – could have anything in common with them. But we listened patiently as the doctor explained. Dyslexia is not usually spotted early. A kid's inability to study for any length of time, to spell and write correctly, to do simple arithmetic, is taken as lack of attentiveness. But if, God forbid, teachers and parents put pressure on the child, which is common in our country, then dyslexia aggravates. By the time the child reaches his teens, he could be close to being autistic.

'Bless yourselves,' said the doctor, 'that you fought with his teachers to let him be. Do exactly as you did, but do not forget to get Ali off mathematics as soon as he is through Class X.' We stared at her, dumbfounded. We had walked the precipice blindfolded. Now, down on earth, we were paralysed with fear.

In 1993, Swapna was back with the United Nations in Bangkok. Buju, Ali and I joined her for the summer holidays. By now, a pattern was visible. In the hands of a trainer, Ali would swim like a would-be champion. Out on the streets and malls, Buju and he would stuff themselves with food, then run riot over 'my lovely clothes'. I suspect Buju was getting influenced by Ali. They could simply not stop eating, and buying clothes.

Were we Right?

Ali had continued art classes in middle school, but after the dyslexia episode we took his painting much more seriously. Upon our request, the Triveni Kala Kendra very kindly agreed to let him join their art school on a part-time basis. I would drive him down every Saturday and he was clearly enjoying it. But during Swapna's absence, Ali's grades had started to inch downwards again. On her return in 1994, his overall grades started improving and he did very well in his Class X final examination.

The question now arose of Ali's choice of subjects for Classes XI and XII. He was a big boy now and had friends who advised him not to take painting as it might affect his chances of admission into a good college later on. We had to argue with him. Finally, we changed the forms he had already submitted, so as to retain painting as his main subject. In retrospect, I think, this was probably the only correct decision we made about Ali. In January 1995, we were living in a university flat at Cavalry Lines when Ali decided to opt for painting as a main subject for his final school examination.

Ali's first major encounter with death occurred when my cousin, the doctor who always treated his bruises, passed away after bypass surgery at the All India Institute of Medical Sciences (AIIMS). This was a horrendous shock. We were all very fond of him. I, for one, never considered checking out what impact his death had on Ali. My cousin was the one we would run to with every real or imaginary physical disorder. And often, to have a good time, we would sprawl out on his carpet, sipping his generous supply of good whisky and eating kababs, with Buju and Ali all over him. It was hard to accept that he was no more.

By the time Ali got to his board exams, he was running away from me and, although to a much lesser extent, also from

Sketch
Green Horse
1997

Swapna. He was immersed in his friends, his football, and his painting. However, with some supervision and help with preparations, there was no major problem with exams. Ali surprised himself by scoring high in humanities with painting as one of his majors. He got admission into History Honours at the prestigious St. Stephen's College on merit, with an option to join the same college under the sports quota with football. He also qualified in the Delhi College of Arts (DCA) admission test.

Ali was very happy that he had made it on his own to St. Stephens College, preferring it to the DCA. It is possible that the pain and discomfort of having to grow up in an academic community with a very non-academic bent of mind was beginning to take its toll. He wanted to conform to the expectations of society and the community of friends he moved with. Our persuasive powers were totally inadequate to convince him to join the DCA.

'One of the most enjoyable meals I have ever had was at Ali's place, around three in the morning. I often stayed over. Mostly, we'd stay awake all night, listening to music, smoking. He'd paint at other times. Once, around dawn, Swapna *Mashi*, Ali's mother, walked into our room. The three of us sat and listened to side B of 'American Beauty' through the quiet winter dawn. It was amazing.'

—Surya

Cow
Watercolour

Ali Finds Himself: Art at Last

That is when Mr Gopi Gajwani, the artist, came to our rescue. A common friend helped us to fix an appointment with Mr Gajwani. Ali was apprehensive about the fact that painting was a risky profession. There was no knowing if he had the talent within to excel at it.

'What if I turn out to be a third-rate artist?' Ali asked.

'What if you turn out to be a third-rate historian?' Mr Gajwani shot back. 'Think of what you would like to do, and let the future take its own course.' Ali chose the Delhi College of Arts (DCA).

This was a totally new and unexpected environment for us. Talented boys and girls with no semblance of discipline or order were about, although much later we understood that there was an undercurrent of discipline. But Ali paid no heed. Let out of school and free to do his paintings and pursue his ideas, he was cutting classes and missing assignments unknown to us. In the first year and a half he adamantly refused to take a ride in his mother's office car that would pass by in front of DCA every day at 9.30 a.m. He fell for the Bohemian style of DCA, hook, line and sinker and got into God knows what vices. He would come home every day either with shining or gloomy eyes, but always to stay home. And he would play pranks, mostly to tease his mother. He came home one day with an earring dangling from one ear, and when his mother protested, he yanked it off. It was a clip on! He grew a French beard and shaved it off. He wore funky casuals and changed to a *kurta pyjama* the next day. But deep inside he continued to be the total child. One day he came home and fell asleep on the carpet in front of the TV when someone called on the phone. I walked up and gave him the cordless, saying, 'Ali, your phone.' God knows what he was dreaming of, the next thing I knew was, eyes still shut, he was trying to eat the phone!

He was clearly moving in with a new circle of friends. Buju was in Bangalore. His friends from school – Tara, Bhrigu, Sanmay, Shiva, Ashok, Chetan, Paroma, Nandini, Arvind – had all moved away. Vandana Madan or Vini, Ali's favourite Vin Din, who was about fifteen years older than him, had been

'I still remember the intense joy I felt at his purposely theatrical amazement on the day when I first showed him that I had worked out parts of Eric Johnson's '*Cliffs of Dover*' on my guitar. I first began playing the guitar to impress Ali as also my father. When both of them died within a year of each other, I found that I didn't enjoy playing that much any more.'

—***Bhrigu***

'He was walking on the ledge of the roof of my house once, when he was in Class XI or XII, I think, swaying his arms, with a bright smile on his face, a little bit drunk, repeating that he was Jim Morrison and saying 'All I wanna do is have my kicks before the whole shithouse goes up in flames.' I was paranoid that he was going to fall off, but he was in control and very happy. He was just getting his kicks.'

—***Sanmay***

our neighbour since his birth, but she had moved out of IEG. Although Ali maintained contact with some of his close friends from school, like Bhrigu and Tara, even they were immersed in their new routines. Ali now had his own to follow. Around the block in Timarpur was a young Sikh lad, Kaka, with whom Ali had made friends and a whole new bunch of boys and girls from DCA. Gautam Kachru was a very close friend. There seemed to be endless get-togethers and parties. Ali would brook no objections from us – he had to go to all of them. And he did. Then came the accident.

Plate 10
Jimi Boy
1998
355 x 520

Plate 11
The Old Man I
1998
Acrylic on canvas
455 x 610

Plate 12
The Old Man II
1998
Acrylic on canvas
455 x 610

Plate 13
Untitled
January, 1998
(City from the Top)
610 x 915

'Ali could withstand huge amounts of pain. One day he landed up with a huge boil on his chin and insisted that we cut it open. Eventually we did; must have been horrendously painful! But immediately afterwards, the skies opened up as in a Shakespearean drama. We all danced in the rain!'

—***Surya and Kapil***

It was an unusually warm November in 1997. We were in the Cavalry Lines flat. The power lines seemed unstable all day, and went out of order with a loud bang in the early evening. Swapna was abroad, attending a meeting. I was waiting for Ali by candlelight, when he came up the rear staircase, followed by Kaka. They were keen to attend a party in south Delhi. Kaka had a Maruti Zen with a driver, said Ali. Both true and false. The driver was absent, so one of the party-goers would drive. I let them go with the standard plea to be careful and not be late. I had dinner and fell asleep.

Voices woke me up, surfacing through a lake filled with waves, 'Professor Mukhopadhyay, Professor Mukhopadhyay, wake up!' Our neighbours were shouting. Buchi was barking. I rushed out. Standing on the stairs, his turban and attire dishevelled, was an elegant Sikh gentleman. 'I am Kaka's father. Arpan has had a terrible accident. Come quickly,' he urged.

So, I shot out. The Maruti 800 I was in was driven by Kaka's father. He kept consoling me, rushing past every traffic light. We arrived at AIIMS at about 4.00 a.m. I was told that the rear of the Maruti Zen, in which five of the kids were travelling, was hit by a speeding truck, which came through a red light at a south Delhi intersection. Two of the five, a girl who was in the driver's seat, and a boy sitting in front, had only minor injuries but the three sitting at the back – Ali, Kaka and Gautam – were blown out by the impact.

I saw Ali lying in one of the emergency alcoves, a mess. I found out later that he had eight fractures, including his right arm and collar and pelvic bones, and an injury to the front lobe of his brain. In the next booth was Gautam, clutching at his knees. He had severe wounds, dangerously close to the spine.

Ali was delirious. He wanted water. He wanted to pee. He wanted to see Kaka. When I had managed to take care of his immediate needs with shouts and bribes, a gentleman in a crumpled suit and reddened eyes walked up to me. 'Are you this boy's relative?' he asked. 'Yes, I am. Who are you?' He was the neurologist.

'I have managed to free one bed,' he said, 'for the other kid. Please take your son away to Apollo or Ganga Ram.' But where

Plate 14
The Skull
March, 1998
Acrylic and ink on canvas
770 x 600

was the other kid? He took me to the far side of Ali's cabin. There, on a table was Kaka, sleeping peacefully. 'He is all right, isn't he?' I asked anxiously. The doctor said nothing, while he quietly pointed at the machine next to Kaka's bed. It was a ventilator.

Kaka died after thirty-six hours.

So, there I was, with a son who had eight major fractures and a brain injury, saddled with the task of transferring him to another hospital. And I did not have my own car!

I called a couple of my ex-students, Smita and Sarat, who had married each other. I was headed for Ganga Ram Hospital, where they had friends. But how would I take Ali there? Were there any ambulances? I was willing to pay for one. 'No sir, only private ones,' came the answer. 'Please get one!' I said.

What came was a tempo van that carried fish and vegetables to the INA market across the road. They had no licence to run this kind of a service. Instead of legalizing them and subjecting them to safety norms, the government had, as usual, declared them to be unauthorized. Being outside the scope of regulations, they followed no norms. I transported my severely injured son on the rocking floor of such a tempo van from AIIMS to Ganga Ram Hospital, holding the drip up in one hand, pushing him against the back of the seat with the other, to keep him from falling.

Smita and Sarat were anxiously waiting for us at Ganga Ram, where Ali would be treated. The scans found a frontal lobe injury in the brain, which we were told 'is likely to heal in time'. Swapna arrived from the airport just in time to hear this report. Ali was transferred to a ward. Little did we know what to expect. A big lad, as strong as an ox, was going full blast in utterly filthy language. His hands and legs had to be tied up, so he screamed and spat at all and sundry. For the next few days and nights, this continued, uninterrupted.

Then, standing by his bed in Ganga Ram, I got the news that my father had passed away in Kolkata. By then, before we realized it, Ali had started to sober down. Vini, whom he loved dearly, was leaving. Having shouted obscenities at her for an hour, Ali burst out, 'Good night, Vini *didi*.' Vini cried.

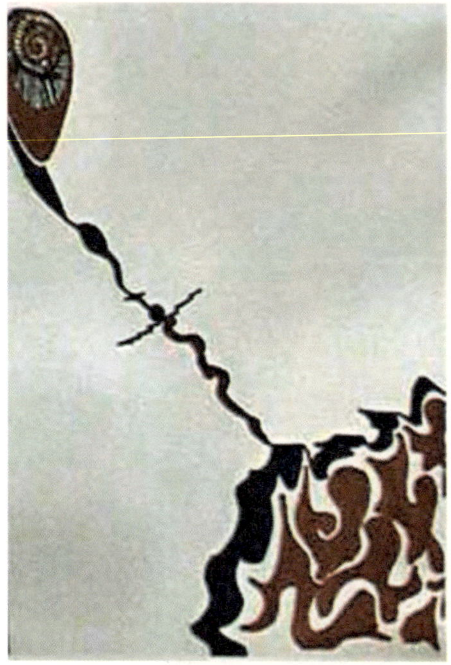

Sketch : ***The Pot Plant***

Sketch : ***Geisha***

Plate 15
Doctor, April, 1998
Acrylic and ink on canvas with mirror
460 x 610

Ganga Ram had a severe shortage of space. After seven days, the doctors decided that Ali was 'out of danger', and wanted to discharge him. We had to bring him home. We were very run down and so, I requested some of my students to help attend to Ali in the night. But in spite of all our precautions, something went wrong.

While all of us were asleep, a friend had called. Ali slept fitfully, because of his head injuries, so he answered the phone. This friend said she felt happy that Ali was back home, unlike Kaka, who had died. Ali did not know this and went into shock. By the time Swapna woke up, he was delirious. He was crying hysterically, attempting to tear off his bandages. We spent the rest of the night trying to hold him down.

Early in the morning, we called Dr A.K. Banerjee, medical superintendent of the R.K. Hospital (across the road from the Mother Dairy Centre) in Patparganj. He was building up this hospital with care and dedication, along with some colleagues, including Dr Mondal, the surgeon who had taken care of Ali at Ganga Ram; they served nearly half their patients charging hardly any fee. Ali spent the next fortnight at this hospital, under the supervision and gentle care of Dr Banerjee and Dr Mondal. Later, while convalescing at home, when his right arm was a little better, Ali sketched Dr Mondal.

Ali slowly recovered at R.K. Hospital. His appetite returned. Our many friends and relatives pitched in to pull us out of the nightmare. My aunt, a fantastic cook, who lived nearby provided a tiffin-carrier full of delicious food for him every day. One particular day, when Swapna and I were totally exhausted, Vini took both of us under her wing, took us home, fed us, and let us sleep and recuperate. She had arranged for an old friend of hers to spend the night at the hospital.

In the midst of all this, our dear friend, the irrepressible Lieutenant General B.S. Malik, persuaded Ali to get rid of his dirty, long hair. He brought a barber to Ali's room in our absence and when we walked in, we were amazed to see this clean young man.

Ali was discharged after two weeks, with strict orders not to get off the bed. We thought this was for his fractures. Later, we realized it was for his brain injuries, which were healing, but very slowly. So, we decided to consult the Vidyasagar Institute of Mental Health and Neurological Sciences (VIMHANS) and its director, Dr A. Banerjee. A series of sessions with him and CAT scans revealed no major damage. We were told we could keep Ali on medication, which was essential for his recovery. But he hated those pills, and after he died, we found a large number of unconsumed capsules under his mattress. He never completed the course.

Back in his room at Cavalry Lines, Ali was compelled to rest on his back in bed for a month. All he saw for a long time was the ceiling fan, so a month later, he sketched the fan. Ali kept thinking of Kaka and the accident – he painted 'The Skull' four weeks later. Ali knew of my great attachment to Satyajit Ray's *Pather Panchali* and painted its lead character, Durga, for me. Most of all, Ali kept mulling over Dr Mondal, who could see through all the X-rays and diagnose accurately.

Ali's wounds began to heal, but there were medical restrictions. The doctors still worried about his brain injury. We bought him a walking stick. Ali would spend hours in the university lawns, leaning on it. He seemed to like his solitary walks, taking stock of life, perhaps making plans for the future. It was at this time that he dropped his bohemian DCA friends. In their place, Ali brought home Surya and Kapil from Kirori Mal College and Shivani and Suchi from Miranda House. Now, that he is gone, we find ourselves trying to reconstruct these memories together.

At the DCA, Ali lost a year. This would have happened even without the accident because he had been absent from too many classes. The pelvic bone injuries and the steel rod in his right arm ruled out playing football. So, Ali concentrated on his friends and his painting. These were not paintings of the type that the college wanted or required, but the way Ali wanted them.

Ali spent a whole day designing the logo for Esha Beteille's Social Science Press. He spent weeks doing graffiti on the walls of his room, some of which survived, thanks to the pictures that his friend, Arun, captured. He spent nights making the two-sided Kandinsky canvas for a play that Bhrigu was directing at St. Stephen's College. At this time, Ali was caught up in a ceaseless spell of sketching and painting.

'Ali used the time in hospital and later on at home, despite plates and a plaster on his right arm, to paint. Ali was trying hard to recover from the trauma of that episode, and for the first time, wasn't looking for our sympathy or attention. I had never really seen this "survivor" side of Ali.'

—Tara

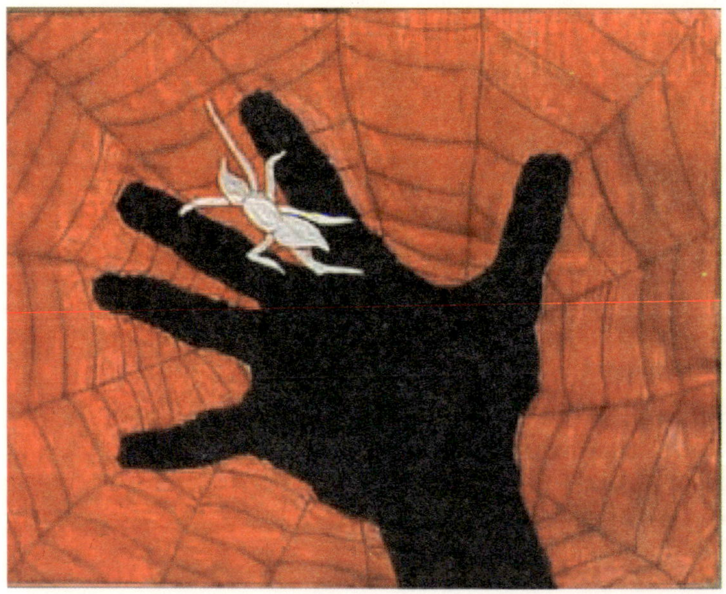

Plate 16
Untitled
December, 1998
Goa Sketch Pad

Plate 17
***Untitled*, 1997**
(Rajasthani Man and Cow)
Etching, 130 x 140

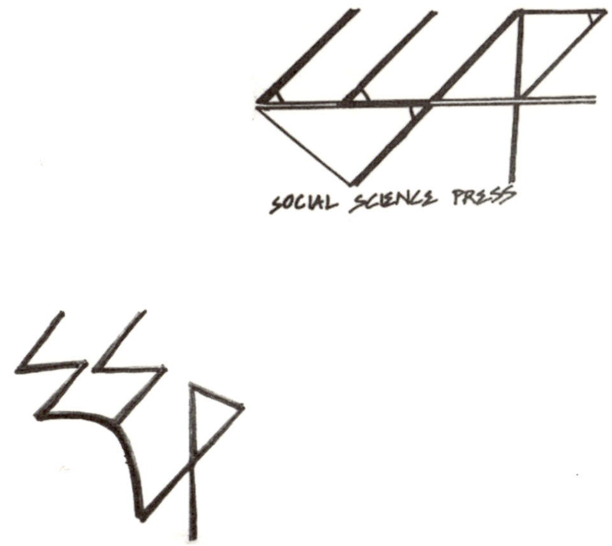

'... One could not set up a publishing outfit without a name and a logo. After a lot of deliberation I decided to call it Social Science Press. But finding the right artist to design a logo was proving to be difficult. Which is when Ali suggested that he would like to try his hand at it. Then followed a series of experiments until he came out with one that seemed to be perfect for the job.'

—***Esha Beteille***

Over the next few months, he worked at a frenzied pace, experimenting with colours, styles and modes, staying up to finish large canvases overnight.

There was one dramatic change in Ali's life at home. He was moving closer to us once more. Unlike earlier times, he did not mind travelling with Swapna to be dropped at DCA, or demonstrating his affection in public. The quality of his friendship did not change, but his choice of friends did. His commitments remained total, often infuriating, but never half-hearted. Ali dropped his earlier associates and bohemian parties. But he continued to work late with Gautam Kachru, who had also recovered, at his house in south Delhi.

By now, Buju had finished his MBA in Bangalore and was working in Mumbai. Early in 1998, Ali planned to visit him for a few days and a ticket was bought for him to travel in the Rajdhani Express.

It was a disaster. Through a massive oversight on the part of all of us, it was late by the time we arrived at the New Delhi Railway Station, and it was uncertain whether Ali would catch the train. Ali jumped out with his backpack before our car stopped and disappeared in the milling crowd. We followed him after parking the car to find that the train had left, and it was impossible to know if Ali had made it at the end. We got announcements made over the public address system for 'Arpan Mukhopadhyay' to meet his parents at the booth, but what we heard was the usual gibberish that no one could make out. After a while, we argued that if he had made it to the train, he would be okay and if not, he would make his way back home, but there was little sense in staying on among the millions in the station. We returned home. We were wrong. Ali missed the train but found a friend, Arun, also desperate to go to Mumbai and also without a ticket for any other train. The two sweet-talked the ticket-checker and got into the Bombay Express. He did have the sense to call us from a public booth to tell us that he was travelling safely. He arrived in Mumbai after thirty-six hours and Buju had no option but to suffer the delay and the stink from Ali's totally dirty clothes.

Sketch
Durga in Pather Panchali
December, 1997
Waterproof ink on transparency
145 x 210

'Ali had begun to keep a sketch pad made of hand-made paper which he would take with him everywhere and draw on. He took it with him to Mumbai in late December where he'd gone for his brother's wedding. From Mumbai he went to Goa.'

—Badal

Buju's Wedding

Late in December 1998, two days before Buju's wedding, we were expecting some relatives who were coming from outside the city. We needed additional space, and took permission from the university to use the empty flat above ours. Late in the evening, just before the big day, I asked Ali to check if everything was working in the flat upstairs. A little later, our cook's son ran in trying to say something in great agitation to Swapna's brother, Khokan. Something was wrong. We rushed upstairs to check.

This is what had happened. After examining the rooms, Ali was checking out the toilet. He was trying to see if the flush attached to an old overhead model of a cast-iron container worked. When Ali pulled the chain, its cover came unstuck and fell on his head, and he was bleeding profusely.

Khokan stopped the bleeding with ice. We rushed Ali to St. Stephen's Hospital for stitches. Throughout the next week, when we were in Mumbai for Buju's marriage ceremonies and in Goa afterwards, Khokan was there to replace the bandage on Ali's forehead daily. I, for one, failed to read the message. In the punch and counterpunch with fate, this kid had always come out a winner. So fate, never a loser, had to change strategy. It did.

Once Buju's wedding festivities were over, the bride and bridegroom left for Kolkata to visit my ailing mother. We all took off for Goa – Ali, Swapna and I, my brother-in-law and sister-in-law with their families, a party of seven. It was a glorious holiday, riotous with colour, fun and food. Most of Ali's sketches reflect this. But it was also the time of year when north India is shrouded in mist and fog. Trains ran between six and fourteen hours late. We had to spend a whole day in the waiting room at Mumbai, on our way back from Goa to Delhi. So Ali sketched the waiting room.

Plate 18
Untitled, December, 1998
(The Tree of Fire)
Goa Sketch Pad

Plate 19
Untitled
December, 1998
Goa Sketch Pad

Plate 20
Untitled
Watercolour on paper

Facing page:
Plate 21
Untitled
Goa Sketch Pad

Facing page:
Plate 22
Untitled
(The Sea), December, 1998
Goa Sketch Pad

Plate 23
Untitled
Goa Sketch Pad
Poster colour on canvas
921 x 1220

Plate 24
The Birds
1999
Acrylic on fibreglass

Plate 25
Untitled
Goa Sketch Pad
Poster colour on canvas
921 x 1220

Next Page:
Plate 26
Untitled, January, 1999
Goa Sketch Pad

Previous page:
Plate 27
Untitled
(The Face),
December, 1998
Goa Sketch Pad

Plate 28
Kermit, 1997
Acrylic and ink
on canvas
610 x 460

Photograph of Ali's table with the Kermit installation
Kermit*, *1997

Plate 29
Untitled (Abstract),
1998
Acrylic on canvas
921 x 1220

Plate 30
Ali-en,
1991
181 x 223

'As a child grows up, he learns automatically to protect himself from undue physical harm. Through the years that Ali was growing up, I would be paralysed with fear for him because he seemed to have no sense of fear that would, ordinarily, act as a deterrent to harming himself. Over the years I realized that he was not going to change: that it was me who would have to learn to live with it, and I did ... to the best of my ability.'

—Ma

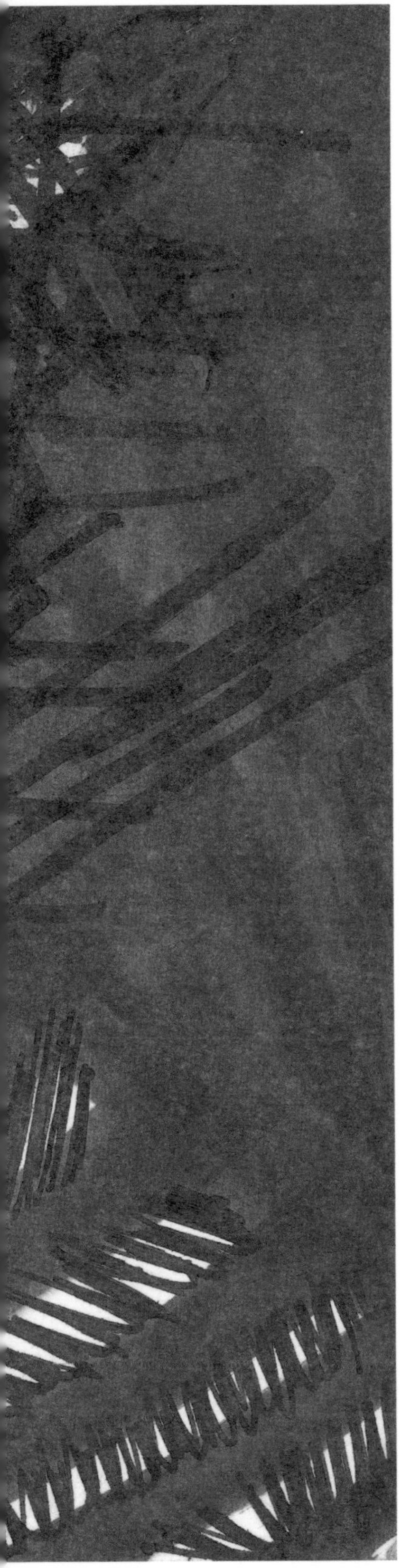

Plate 31
Untitled
December, 1998
Goa Sketch Pad

Death

Back in Delhi, we tried to settle into some semblance of a routine. On the evening of 27 January 1999, Ali came home from DCA with a high submission grade. He wanted to be with his friends at KMC. 'Do not be late for dinner!' I remember calling out. But he was. At about 8.00 p.m., he came back to say that he would have dinner with his friends. Swapna asked him to bring his friends over to dinner, but he disagreed. They had already made other arrangements – he would join them for dinner, then return home by himself.

We tried to reconstruct the happenings of that night. We now know that, after dinner, Ali spent time with his friends, then took an auto-rickshaw that probably dropped him home at about 1.00 a.m. He must have let himself in and fallen asleep on his bed. His room was stacked with woollen rugs and acrylic-filled sleeping bags to accommodate his friends, mainly from the surrounding college hostels, who might stay over for the night. Either the electrical lines, or the candles he was using for a light-and-shade effect on his last unfinished piece of work, or a carelessly thrown cigarette butt, had set something on fire within his room. The synthetic sleeping material emitted dangerous fumes of carbon monoxide. Buchi managed to survive – she must have breathed in air from under the door. But Ali peacefully sank to his death.

It was a stormy night of shadows. Early in the morning, when Swapan burst into the door, she could see nothing because of the smoke. As mists and fog swirled over the roads, I drove Ali to the casualty ward of St. Stephen's Hospital. A young intern with bloodshot eyes took one look at him and shouted at the nurse for an ECG of the wrist. I saw the angriest growl of fate, a flat red line on the monitor. Ali was dead of monoxide poisoning. Having hit him over and over again, and failed each time, fate just put him to sleep.

A thirty-one-point hand comes once in about two million deals. Funny, most parents who get them, do not recognize them, then go through life with no compunction. Yet a few hapless fools get a thirty-one-point hand, see it, and throw it away.

'What shall we use to fill the empty spaces
Where we used to talk?
How shall I fill the final places?
How can I complete the wall?'

'Empty Spaces', Pink Floyd

Plate 32
Untitled
December, 1998
Goa Sketch Pad

Plate 33
Kandinsky, Side 1
October, 1998
Acrylic on canvas
921 x 1220

Plate 34
Kandinsky, Side 2
Acrylic on canvas
921 x 1220

Plate 35
The Train Derailed
January, 1999
Acrylic on canvas
with mirror
921 x 1220

‘Ali loved to hide
away faces in some
of his later paintings.’

—***Anirban***

Plate 36
Untitled

Plate 37
Tales of Mystery and Imagination
April, 1998
Acrylic and ink on canvas
765 x 1220

"TALES OF MYSTERY AND IMAGINATION"

→ This painting which is done in Acrylic medium with a comb to give the textured surface and with ink finishing is about a dream, I dreamt.

From a distance it looks like a Rajasthani "Jooti" or sandal which takes the form of a traveller holding a wand. The faces seen – that of a cat, owls, dogs, fish, chicken a skull, a wizard are all memories or vague glances of faces which I, the "Traveller" saw in my dream, in my state of subconsciousness.

A dream is a dream and I feel it needs no definition – Neither does a painting. After all, it's a feeling, an expression.

THE REST IS FOR YOU TO SEE.

ali.

The above note on the painting was written by Ali: one of the very few descriptions he has left of his work.
April, 1998

Plate 38
Untitled
(Abstract, red and white)

Plate 39
Untitled (Intersecting Circles)

Plate 40
Untitled (Abstract Eye)

Plate 41
Untitled
(Seated in Garden)

Plate 42
Heart of the Sun

Plate 43
Untitled

Plate 44
Untitled (Abstract, black and white)

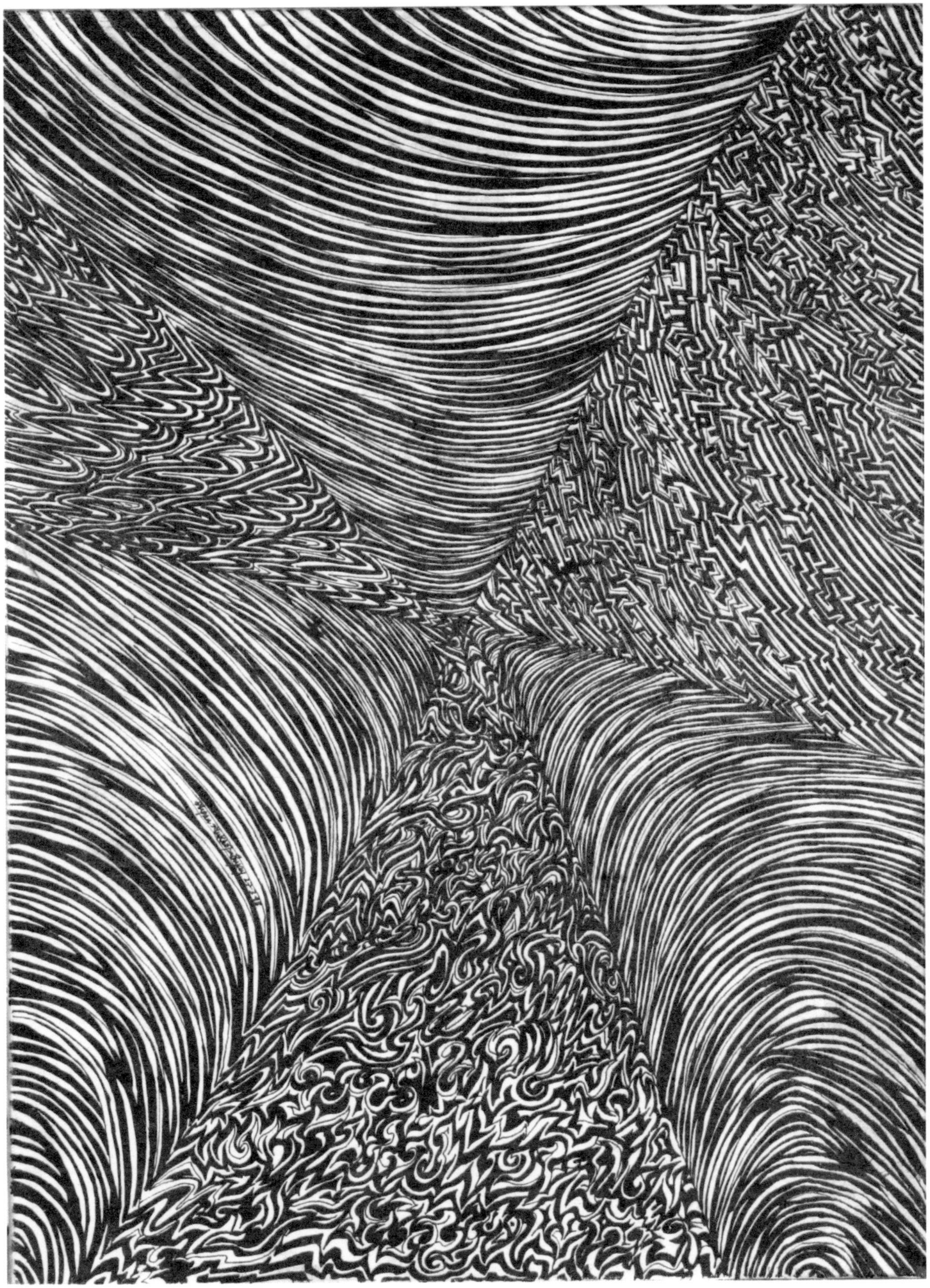

Plate 45
The Fan
March, 1998
Acrylic and ink
on canvas
610 x 460

Plate 46
The Moon and Two Towers 1998
Acrylic and ink on canvas
460 x 608
The two towers were Kapil's contribution

***Untitled*, 1995**
Acrylic on paper
460 x 608

Acknowledgements

Acknowledging debts in a book like this is not a routine formality. As the parents of a lost child, we feel indebted not only to those who made the book possible but also to those who made the child happy. In Ali's case, fortunately, there is a large overlap between the two groups but yet, since he was such a friendly soul, we are sure to miss out on many of his friends. That we regret.

First, those that helped him to live, and function – for as long as he did. Dr S Kavan of St. Stephen's Hospital was responsible for Ali being alive. Dr Sarla Khanvilkar, paediatrician in the same hospital, nurtured him out of serious danger – and became a friend. Our late cousin Dr V. Chatterjee, Chief Medical Officer of the Indo-Tibetan Border Police (ITBP), who, till 1995, when he himself passed away, tolerated and treated every possible broken bone and misadventure of the kid. Dr A. Banerjee of R.K. Hospital flooded us with his kindness when Ali had to be hospitalized a second time after a deadly car accident in 1997. Dr. Mondal (whom he painted) was the key to his recovery at the time.

Ali was not quite a teachers' pet. But the teachers in Shiv Niketan, Aunty Gauba, and her unparalleled team of teachers, who had spotted that he 'liked to smell orange-scented erasers', without whose love and care this dyslexic child could easily have regressed to autism, all had a hand in making him what he became. We would also like to express our gratitude to Mrs Rani Sarma of Springdales School and Mr Vijay Mohan of the Delhi College of Arts who won the heart of this restless child and treated him with the love and patience that he dearly needed.

Ali was an out-going, friendly and generous soul. He was very popular among his friends, who came from all ages and stations in life. It would be difficult, perhaps impossible, to name all but there are some we cannot but mention. Vini, next to Tara, was privy to Ali's thoughts as he was growing up. Bhrigu and Sanmay were partners in the trio that spent countless number of days together. There were many more, we know, but unfortunately far too numerous to mention.

The idea of a book had lurked in our mind for a long time. The beginning was made in January 2000, a year after Ali had passed away, when many of his friends, Bhrigu, Prerna, Surjo, Shivani, Kapil, Suchi, Deba, Tiya, Vini, Gautam, Abhijit and others who had helped us put up an exhibition of his paintings at the India Habitat Centre, also decided that we make a book of his paintings. At that time, Priya Khanna and Priya Arora, two of his seniors at the Delhi College of Arts, had spent an enormous amount of time restoring the paintings damaged by smoke in Ali's bedroom the night he died. Arun, along with Gautam, laboured for ages taking digital photographs of his paintings. And then those photographs were scrutinized, washed, polished, sorted, computerized, by Kapil, Suchi, Saugata, and who knows who else? Ali lived for his friends. And the friends came together when we needed them. But it was Tara, of course, who held our hands and gave us the courage to get started on this book. So Tara shares responsibility with us for all its defects.

But perhaps no one put in more into the book than Rajashi, our dear niece (Popla), who conceptualized the original design and helped us get the actual work on the book off the ground. Stationed abroad, she had not seen Ali in his later years. Since she felt that as the designer of the book she needed to know him inside out, Popla framed an elaborate questionnaire which we had to send to a number of Ali's friends across the world. We were overwhelmed by the response. We are grateful to Advait, Rahul, Tara, Vini, Bhrigu, Sanmay, Saugata, Surjo and Aniket, among others, for penning down memories of their friend. Excerpts from some of these responses occur through the book. Later on, Buju and Sujata, our elder son and daughter-in-law, as well as Tara, went through several versions

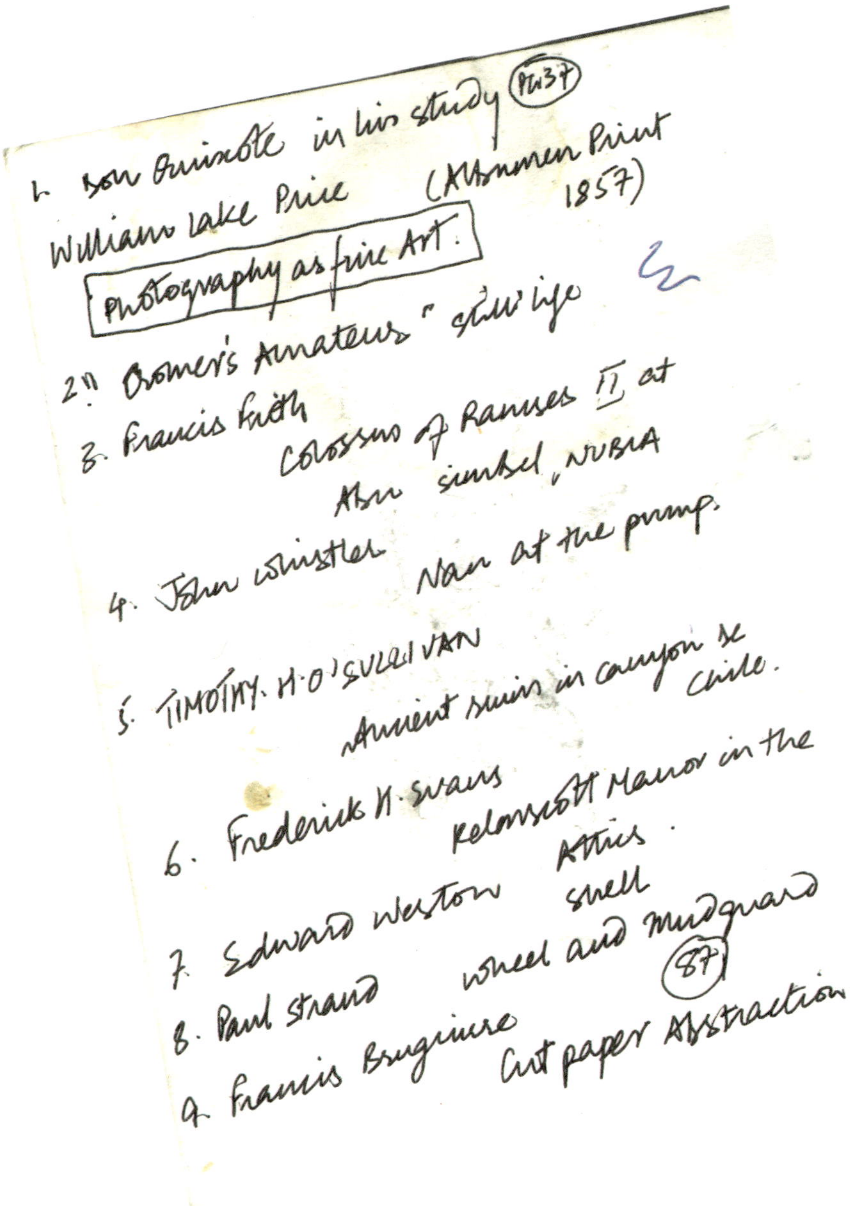

1. Don Quixote in his study (Pl. 37)
William Lake Price (Albumen Print 1857)
Photography as fine Art.
2" Bromer's Amateurs " still life
3. Francis Frith Colossus of Ramses II at Abu Simbel, NUBIA
4. John Whistler Nan at the pump.
5. TIMOTHY. H. O'SULLIVAN Ancient ruins in canyon de Chile.
6. Frederick H. Evans Kelmscott Manor in the Attics.
7. Edward Weston Shell
8. Paul Strand Wheel and Mudguard (87)
9. Francis Bruguiere Cut paper Abstraction

of the manuscript, detecting errors of omission and commission. Our other precious niece, Rekha, better known as Aditi De in the world of art critics, and Esha Beteille of the Social Science Press, Ali's favourite Esha Mashi, pitched in with their editorial skills. We would also like to thank our dear friend, the irrepressible Keya Kullar, who has helped us greatly with her valuable help and advice. Many others who have helped us in the process of putting this book together would have gone unnamed. Our sincere apologies.

The project was stalled for many months in between while we searched in vain for a sensitive, competent and honest designer who could sort through a large amount of material and put the stray components together in order to give the book its final form within the broad structure conceptualized by Popla. At times when things started to look bleak, it was Ali's friends once again, Kapil and Suchi in particular, who had helped keep our spirits up. In the end, things worked out beautifully. We were hugely fortunate to find an answer to our prayers in the person of Neelima Rao, the gifted young designer who, as a bonus for us, also happens to be a wonderful human being.

Our sincere gratitude also goes out to Pramod and Priya Kapoor and the team of competent workers at Roli Books, the Publishers and Distributors of the book, for their generous help.

Buju, who had to bear with his mischievous younger brother throughout his growing up years, has been like a rock of support from a distance during the entire period the book had been shaping up, helping us with his advice and his views, always thoughtful and measured.

We share this book with all those who, unknown to one another, have journeyed through the same private grief as we have, towards the same abode of tranquillity we all seek. We dedicate this book to the numerous friends of Ali's, young and old, who touched his life at some point of time or the other, in some capacity or the other, and loved him for what he was.

The painting lies unfinished
A few brush strokes on a half-filled canvas
From he who has crossed the twilight
More colours on his palette than a rainbow can hold
Coaxed and charmed into ... what?
The frozen image of a passing thought?
In searing flames now lies asleep
Pray to the world his soul to keep
'Ali', God's chosen one now lies
As 'Arpan', an offering to the skies.

—Mohammed Adil, 28 January, 1999

List of Plates

Plate 01
Page 6

Plate 02
Page 9

Plate 03
Page 10

Plate 04
Page 11

Plate 05
Page 16

Plate 06
Page 23

Plate 07
Page 32

Plate 08
Page 33

Plate 09
Page 34

Plate 10
Page 39

Plate 11
Page 40

Plate 12
Page 41

Plate 13
Page 42

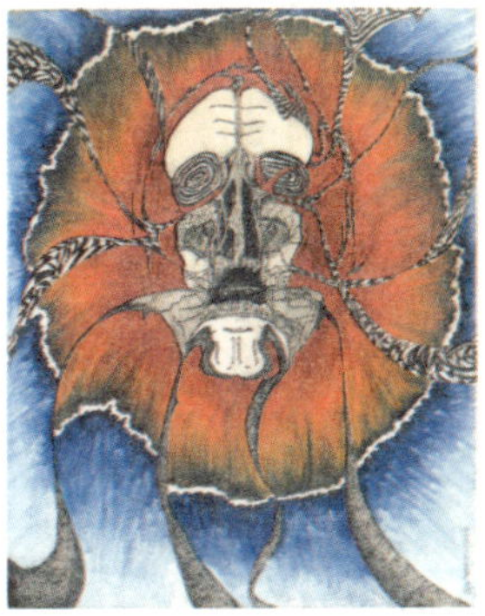
Plate 14
Page 44

Plate 15
Page 47

Plate 16
Page 49

Plate 17
Page 50

Plate 18
Page 53

Plate 19
Page 54

Plate 20
Page 54

Plate 21
Page 55

Plate 22
Page 56

Plate 23
Page 57

Plate 24
Page 58

Plate 25
Page 59

Plate 26
Page 60

Plate 27
Page 61

Plate 28
Page 62

Plate 29
Page 64

Plate 30
Page 65

Plate 31
Page 68

Plate 32
Page 71

Plate 33
Page 72

Plate 34
Page 73

Plate 35
Page 74

Plate 36
Page 75

Plate 37
Page 76

Plate 38
Page 78

Plate 39
Page 79

Plate 40
Page 80

Plate 41
Page 81

Plate 42
Page 82

Plate 43
Page 83

Plate 44
Page 84

Plate 45
Page 85

Plate 46
Page 86

ISBN: 978-81-7436-674-0

This edition published in 2008 by Roli Books
M-75 Greater Kailash II (Market),
New Delhi 110 048, India
Ph: ++91-11-29212782, 29210886
Fax: ++91-11-29217185
E-mail: roli@vsnl.com
Website: rolibooks.com

Graphic Design: Rajashi Ghosh, Neelima Rao • Editor: Dipali Singh
Production: Naresh Nigam, Kumar Raman

Printed and bound in India by Gopsons Papers Ltd., Noida 201301